HOW to DRAW CUTE STUFF for kidS

Lyra Lee

Table of Content

Nature&Scenery.

Yummy Foods

yummm!

Hello. I'm Lyra's Dad. Inspired by my daughter's love of drawing, I made "How to Draw Cute Stuff" to enjoy together!

This book is designed for beginners and aims to help you explore the joy of drawing cute stuff. As you flip through the pages, think about each cute stuff and how you can bring it to life with your unique touch.

I hope your creativity flourishes as we learn and improve our drawing skills.

How to use this book?

●••••••••••••••••••••••••••••••●

"How to Draw Cute Stuff." This book is divided into 5 sections (Fantasy Creatures, School, Fun Objects, Nature & Scenery, and Yummy Foods). It consists of 52 stuff that children like and want to draw.

Each stuff comes with simple step-by-step instructions to make it easy and enjoyable. Even beginners can draw along easily.

Drawing levels are divided into three: Easy, Normal, and Hard. If you want to build confidence in drawing, I recommend starting with EASY.

here are subtle differences between e-books and paperbacks. Both offer step-by-step guides, but the paperback includes a "Practice" section where you can draw the whole picture and a "Drawing and Coloring" section where you can redraw and color it in your own style.

① **Step-by-Step Guide**
(E-Book&Paperback)

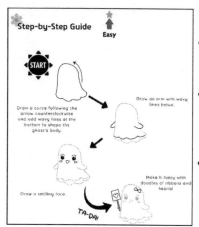

- **Learn** to draw by following the guide
- **The black lines** are the start of each step
- The gray lines are the steps before.

② **Practice**
(Paperback only)

- Get confidence to draw by drawing along the gray line of the whole picture

③ **Drawing and Coloring**
(Paperback only)

- Draw and Color **your "cute stuff"**

—♥—♥—♥—♥—♥—♥—♥—♥—♥—♥—♥—♥—♥—♥—(

Tools

You don't need to buy or prepare a lot of tools to draw cute stuff. Just get a few basic supplies and get ready to create amazing artwork!

<Pencil>

The pencil is a versatile and essential tool for any artist. It helps you create detailed and precise lines. Remember, you don't have to draw perfectly with a pencil right from the start. Keep a pencil sharpener nearby. So, grab your pencil and get ready to draw some cute stuff!

<Eraser>

Don't forget the eraser either. It's your secret weapon for fixing those little sketching mistakes and making your drawings even better!

<Paper>

You can use any notebook or paper you have at home, but be careful with printer paper when coloring with markers, as the ink can bleed through and damage the next page. I recommend using a sketchbook the most.

<Marker&Color Pencil>

It's a good idea to mix 2 to 3 colors when coloring. A 24-pack of colored pencils is enough. Markers are great for showing different colors and can also create shadow effects. When using markers, I recommend using thick paper to prevent smudging or bleeding through.

Tips

These tips will help you build confidence in your drawing. Each one is made to guide you through the basics and inspire you to keep getting better.

<Basic - lines and shapes>

When you follow a step-by-step guide, there are certain lines and shapes you draw often. Practice drawing the basic lines and shapes below on a sketchbook or blank paper.

[1] Wavy lines

General wavy line

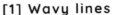

Titled wavy line   Wavy line shape

[Axolotl ears]

[Aloe Vera planter]

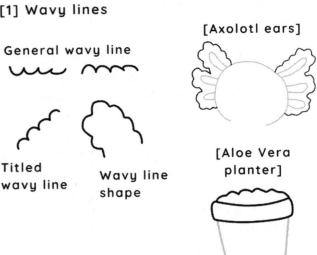

[2] Zigzag lines

Square zigzag lines

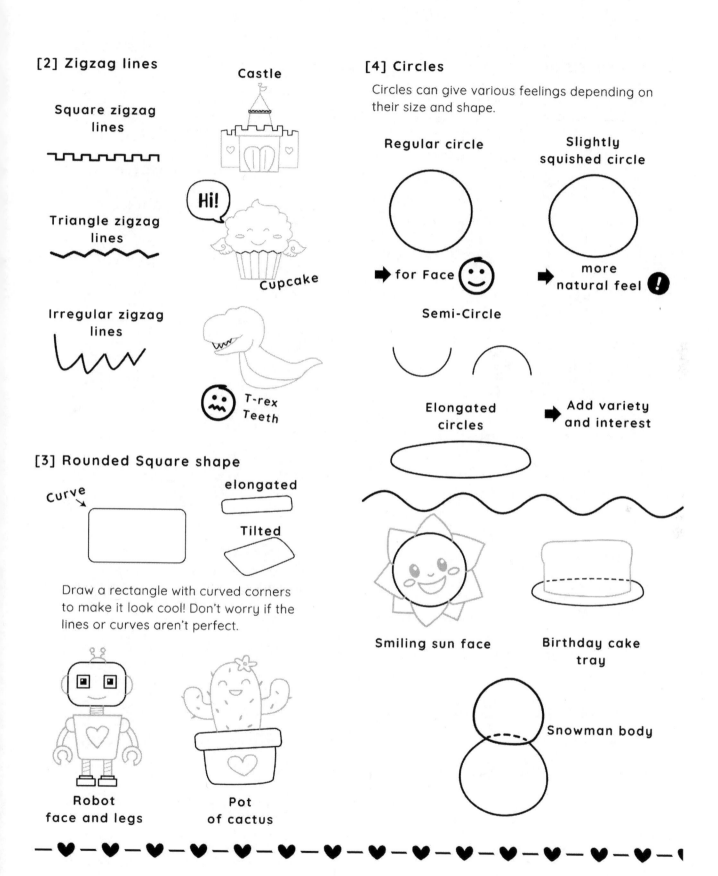

Castle

Triangle zigzag lines

Hi!

Cupcake

Irregular zigzag lines

T-rex Teeth

[3] Rounded Square shape

Curve

elongated

Tilted

Draw a rectangle with curved corners to make it look cool! Don't worry if the lines or curves aren't perfect.

Robot face and legs

Pot of cactus

[4] Circles

Circles can give various feelings depending on their size and shape.

Regular circle

Slightly squished circle

➡ for Face

➡ more natural feel ❗

Semi-Circle

Elongated circles

➡ Add variety and interest

Smiling sun face

Birthday cake tray

Snowman body

<Face : expression>

You can make your drawings more fun by adding different expressions from Cute Stuff at the end. Try drawing many faces with various emotions! I'll give you three tips for facial expressions. Use these tips to create adorable characters with lots of different looks.

[1] Smiling

Eyebrows and mouths are usually drawn as semicircles. Add ovals under the eyes to make the face even cuter!

Smiling Ghost   Smiling Peach

[2] Suprised

Draw a sideways triangle for surprised eyes. For the mouth, draw a "3" turned on its side.

yummy donuts   Aloe Vera

[3] Pretty

Draw two or three curved lines next to the eyes, pointing up toward the eyebrows, to show eyelashes.

Pretty Unicorn   Pretty Mermaid

The Cute STUFF Collection

14 Normal — Axolotl

16 Hard — Dragon

18 Easy — Ghost

20 Normal — Mermaid

22 Normal — Mermaid tail

24 Hard — T-Rex

26 Normal — Unicorn

28 Normal — Unicorn face

30 Normal — Backpack

32 Normal — Clock

34 Easy — Eraser

Easy : Basic Shapes   Normal : Shapes + Curve   Hard : Many Curves

-9- Collection

36 Easy — Marker

38 Normal — Mug

40 Easy — Soap

42 Easy — Camp fire

44 Easy — Candle

46 Normal — Hot air balloon

48 Easy — Lipstick

50 Easy — Magic Wand

52 Normal — Phone

54 Hard — Robot

56 Normal — Airplane

Easy : Basic Shapes   Normal : Shapes + Curve   Hard : Many Curves

Easy : Basic Shapes   Normal : Shapes + Curve

78 Normal
Snowman

80 Normal
Avocado

82 Easy
Banana

84 Normal
Birthday cake

86 Normal
Burger

88 Easy
Carrot

90 Normal
Cherry

92 Normal
Chocolate

94 Hard
Cupcake

96 Easy
Dango

Easy : Basic Shapes   Normal : Shapes + Curve   Hard : Many Curves

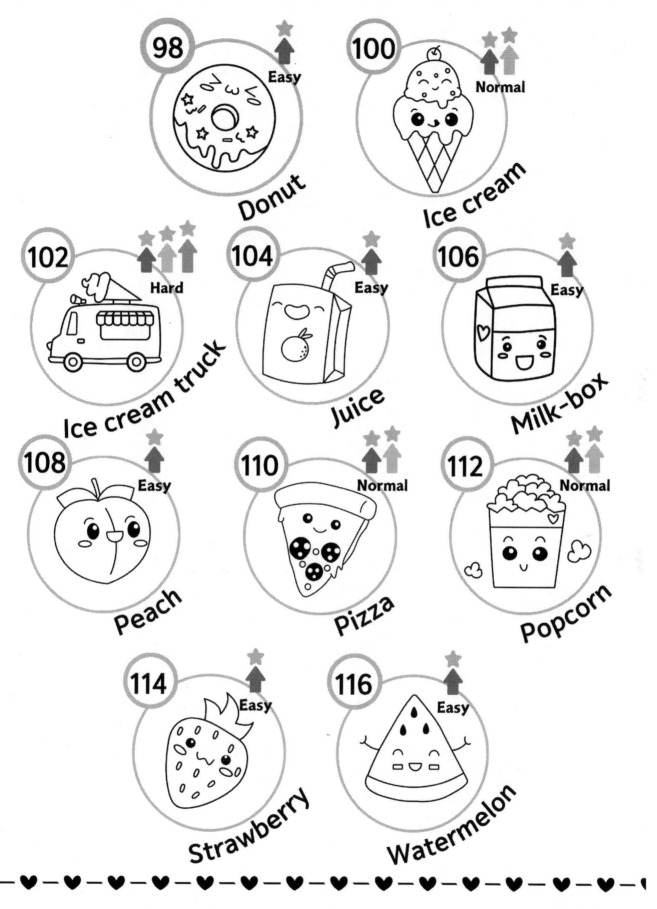

98 Easy **Donut**

100 Normal **Ice cream**

102 Hard **Ice cream truck**

104 Easy **Juice**

106 Easy **Milk-box**

108 Easy **Peach**

110 Normal **Pizza**

112 Normal **Popcorn**

114 Easy **Strawberry**

116 Easy **Watermelon**

Easy : Basic Shapes Normal : Shapes + Curve Hard : Many Curves

Axolotl

Step-by-Step Guide

Normal

1

Draw an incomplete circle.

2

Draw 6 half ovals of different lengths next to the face.

3

Draw a wavy line surrounding the ear.

4

Draw curves to create arms. Draw straight lines on the arms to represent fingernails.

5

One curve starts from the arms, and another starts from the face and curves down to complete the feet.

6

Draw a pretty face. Draw the tail and erase the part that overlaps the feet.

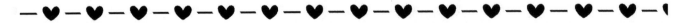

Axolotl

Practice

Draw the entire picture (gray line) following the step-by-step guide

 Drawing and Coloring

Dragon

Step-by-Step Guide

Hard

1 Draw a circle.

2 Draw a triangle with a curved line on the top of the face, then add curves on each side to complete the ears.

3 Create arms with a long curved line under the face. Draw a wavy line inside the arm.

4 Draw curved and wavy lines as indicated to complete the wings. Add additional lines inside.

5 Complete the legs by drawing an oval shape connecting to the arms. Add several curved lines between the arms.

6 Draw a cute face.

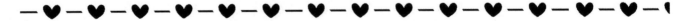

Dragon

Drawing and Coloring

— ♥ — ♥ — ♥ — ♥ — ♥ — ♥ — ♥ — ♥ — ♥ — ♥ — ♥ — ♥ — ♥ —

Ghost

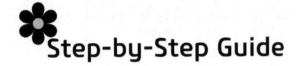 **Step-by-Step Guide**

Easy

START

Draw a curve following the arrow counterclockwise and add wavy lines at the bottom to shape the ghost's body.

Draw an arm with wavy lines below.

Draw a smiling face.

Make it fancy with doodles of ribbons and hearts!

TA-DA!

Ghost

Practice

Draw the entire picture (gray line) following the step-by-step guide

Drawing and Coloring

Mermaid

🌸 Step-by-Step Guide

Normal

1

Draw a semicircle, then add a triangular line that covers it.

2

Finish the ears with semicircles and the hair with curved lines around the face.

3

Draw a line under the face, add long lines on each side, and finish the arms with small zigzag lines.

4

1. Draw an "8" shape.
2. Add lines to draw the body.
3. Complete the skirt with wavy lines.

5

Draw two long curves going down and connect them. Complete the tail with 6 long ovals and add wavy lines inside.

6

Draw a pretty face. Draw a ribbon and decorate it as well.

— ♥ — ♥ — ♥ — ♥ — ♥ — ♥ — ♥ — ♥ — ♥ — ♥ — ♥ — ♥ — ♥ —

Mermaid

Practice

Draw the entire picture (gray line) following the step-by-step guide

Drawing and Coloring

Mermaid tail
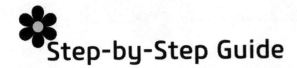

🌸 Step-by-Step Guide

Normal

1

Draw two wavy lines and connect them.

2

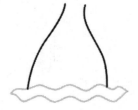

Draw two curves.

3

Draw a curve in the direction of the arrow and connect it with a wavy line to complete the fin.

4

Draw a curve at the thinnest point and connect each bend of the fin with a line.

5

Draw several semicircles inside the tail.

6

Draw several circles on the outside of the tail.

Mermaid tail

Practice

Draw the entire picture (gray line) following the step-by-step guide

Drawing and Coloring

T-Rex

Step-by-Step Guide

Hard

1

Complete the face by drawing curves in the order of the arrows. Draw some wavy lines on the top of the face.

2

Create the T-Rex's teeth by drawing several triangular zigzag lines.

3

Draw two curved lines starting from the bottom of the body, connect them, and draw an inner line

4

Draw a curved line on the left side of the body and make a claw in the shape of a triangle.

5

Draw a half oval from the body, add lines for the feet, and draw the claws. Erase any lines that overlap the body.

6

Draw a cute face and add several semicircles to the body.

T-Rex

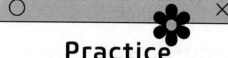

Practice

Draw the entire picture (gray line) following the step-by-step guide

Drawing and Coloring

UniCorn

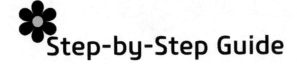

Step-by-Step Guide

Normal

1

Draw a semicircle and add several curved lines to complete the head.

2

Add two semicircles to the sides of the head to make ears and draw horns.

3

Draw a cute and pretty unicorn face.

4

Create the arms by drawing two curved lines and adding lines inside.

5

Draw two curved lines next to the arms and connect the circles. Draw a straight line between the arms.

6

Draw a wavy line to make a tail.

UniCorn

Practice

Draw the entire picture (gray line) following the step-by-step guide

Drawing and Coloring

Unicorn face

🌸 Step-by-Step Guide

Normal

1

Draw a curve in the direction of the arrow.

2

Add a wavy line to the top of the face to draw hair.

3

Add a half oval and draw additional hair with several curves.

4

Draw curved lines to complete the rest of the hair.

5

Make a unicorn horn and crown.

6

Draw a cute face. Adding a star next to the face makes it even cooler!

Unicorn face

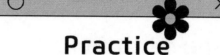

Practice

Draw the entire picture (gray line) following the step-by-step guide

Drawing and Coloring

Backpack

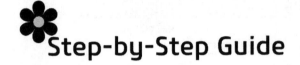

❀ **Step-by-Step Guide**

Normal

①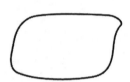

Draw a square shape with rounded ends. The upper right corner is finished with a round curve.

②

Draw two curves starting from the right. Add a line inside.

③

Connect the remaining curves. Draw a square inside.

④

Draw a cute face.

⑤

Draw a semicircle and add a smaller semicircle inside. For the right bag strap, draw a large semicircle (1) and a curved line inside (2) and a long curve down (3).

⑥

Draw a semicircle and draw an additional curve.

Backpack

Practice

Draw the entire picture (gray line) following the step-by-step guide

Drawing and Coloring

CloCk

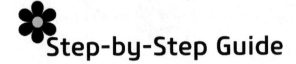

Step-by-Step Guide

Normal

1

Draw a large circle and draw a small circle inside.

2

Connect the lines on the circle and draw a semicircle. Then, add a small semicircle above it.

3

Connect the half-square shape with rounded ends above and below the large circle.

4

Draw the clock hours and minutes.

5

Draw a pretty face.

6

Draw 12 lines inside a small circle.

CloCk

Practice

Draw the entire picture
(gray line) following
the step-by-step guide

Drawing and Coloring

Eraser

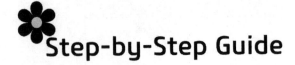

✿ **Step-by-Step Guide**

Easy

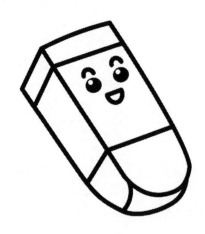

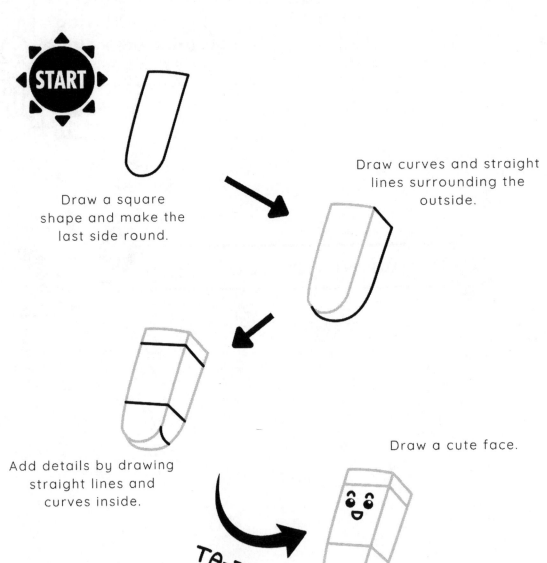

START

Draw a square shape and make the last side round.

Draw curves and straight lines surrounding the outside.

Add details by drawing straight lines and curves inside.

TA-DA!

Draw a cute face.

Eraser

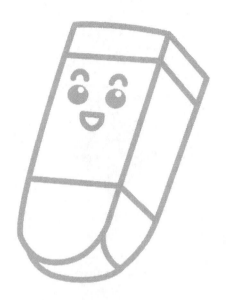

Practice

Draw the entire picture (gray line) following the step-by-step guide

Drawing and Coloring

Marker

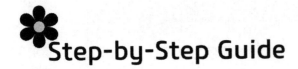

Step-by-Step Guide

Easy

START

Draw a tilted rectangle and add 2 lines inside.

Draw 2 curves and connect them. Draw a square shape with sharp ends.

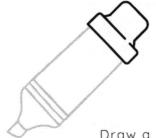

Draw a rectangle and erase part of it. Round the edges and draw a square shape.

Draw a cute face.

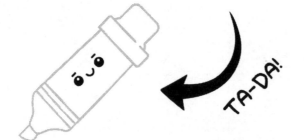

TA-DA!

Marker

Practice

Draw the entire picture (gray line) following the step-by-step guide

Drawing and Coloring

Mug

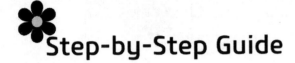

Step-by-Step Guide

Normal

1

Draw an oval.

2

Draw 2 straight lines below the oval and connect them with a curved line.

3

Draw two semicircles to create the shape of ears.

4

Draw a wavy line in the direction of the arrow. This will be the cat's face.

5

Draw a semicircle and add lines to complete the claw. Add triangular lines to create the ears.

6

Draw a cute cat face.

Mug

Practice

Draw the entire picture
(gray line) following
the step-by-step guide

Drawing and Coloring

Soap

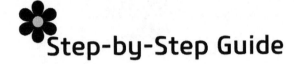

❀ Step-by-Step Guide

Easy

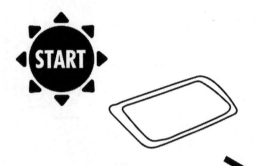

Draw a square shape with rounded ends and a square shape inside.

Draw a line at each vertex and connect the lines.

Draw a cloud shape and place it at the end of the square. Also, draw a ribbon.

TA-DA!

Draw a cute face.

Soap

Practice

Draw the entire picture (gray line) following the step-by-step guide

 Drawing and Coloring

camp fire

❀ Step-by-Step Guide

Easy

START

1

2

Draw a curve counterclockwise and draw a wavy line to resemble a fire.

Draw a small, similar shape inside.

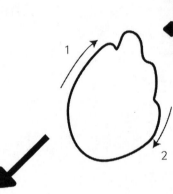

Draw a cute face. Add a water drop shape at the top.

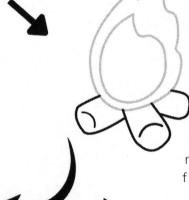

Draw a half-square with rounded ends around the fire and add a curved line inside.

TA-DA!

Camp fire

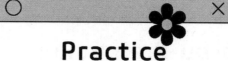

Practice

Draw the entire picture (gray line) following the step-by-step guide

Drawing and Coloring

Candle

Step-by-Step Guide

Easy

START

Draw half-square shapes with sides of different lengths. Connect them with a wavy line at the top.

Draw the remaining curves to connect the wavy lines. Draw a semicircle inside.

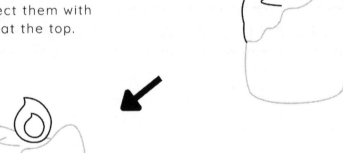

Draw water droplets with sharp tips to create the shape of a candle flame.

TA-DA!

Draw a cute face. Draw and color straight lines and semi-ellipses.

Candle

Practice

Draw the entire picture (gray line) following the step-by-step guide

Drawing and Coloring

Hot air balloon

Step-by-Step Guide

Normal

1

Draw an incomplete circle shaped like a balloon.

2

On the inside, draw curves as if they are converging inside the balloon.

3

Add two wavy lines at the top.

4

Draw a cute face.

5

Draw a long rectangle at the bottom and draw a straight line.

6

Draw rectangles with rounded ends and squares with small lines inside.

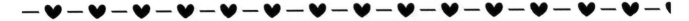

Hot air balloon

Practice

Draw the entire picture (gray line) following the step-by-step guide

Drawing and Coloring

Lipstick

 Step-by-Step Guide

Easy

START

Tilt the oval and draw
two vertical lines.

Draw a half square.

Draw a rectangle with
rounded ends.

Draw a cute face.

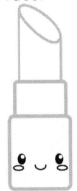

TA-DA!

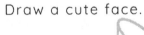

Lipstick

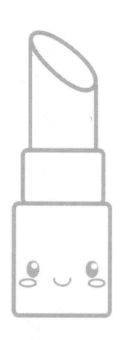

Practice

Draw the entire picture (gray line) following the step-by-step guide

Drawing and Coloring

Magic wand

✿ **Step-by-Step Guide**

Easy

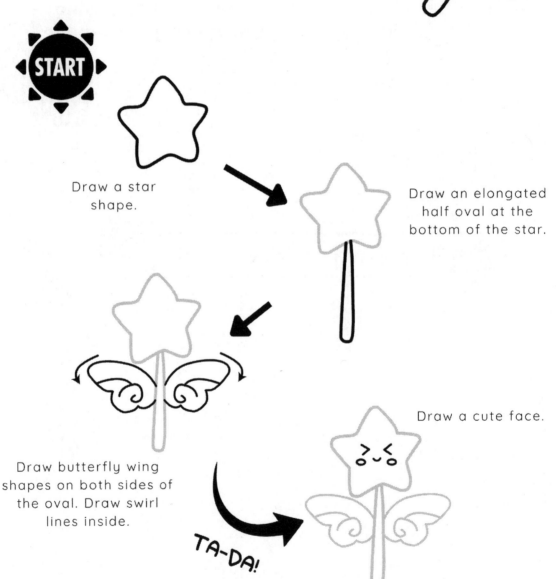

Draw a star shape.

Draw an elongated half oval at the bottom of the star.

Draw butterfly wing shapes on both sides of the oval. Draw swirl lines inside.

TA-DA!

Draw a cute face.

Magic wand

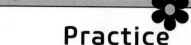

Practice

Draw the entire picture (gray line) following the step-by-step guide

Drawing and Coloring

Phone

Step-by-Step Guide

Normal

1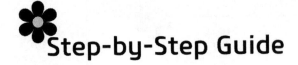

Draw a rectangle with rounded corners at an angle.

2

Draw a ribbon shape at the top.

3

Draw a small square inside the top left corner.

4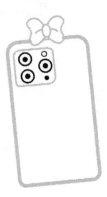

Create a phone camera by drawing a circle and a colored circle inside the square.

5

Draw a speech bubble and heart in the center.

6

Draw a cute face.

Phone

Practice

Draw the entire picture (gray line) following the step-by-step guide

 Drawing and Coloring

Robot

❀ **Step-by-Step Guide**

Hard

1

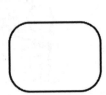

Draw a rectangle with rounded ends.

2

Draw semicircles on the sides and top, and connect the curves and circles to complete the robot's head.

3

Draw a straight line for the neck and a trapezoid for the body.

4

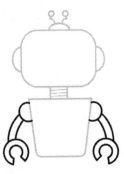

Draw a circle on each side and connect them with curved lines. Create arms by drawing two circles at 2/3 size.

5

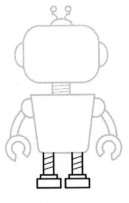

Draw a straight line underneath the body and draw rectangles of different sizes.

6

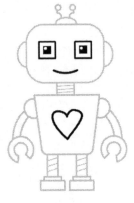

Draw a cute face. Draw a heart in the center.

Robot

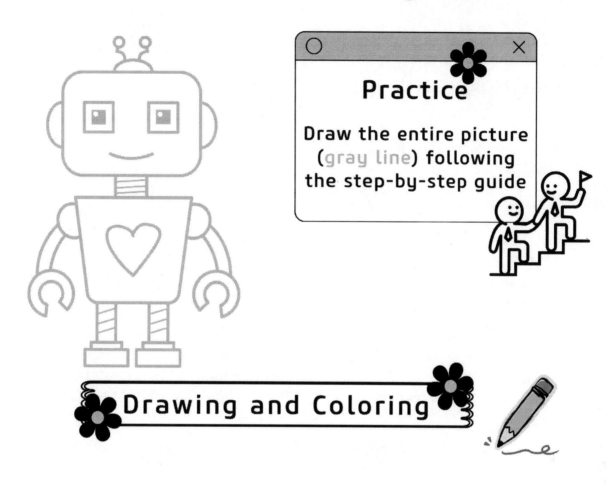

Practice

Draw the entire picture (gray line) following the step-by-step guide

Drawing and Coloring

Airplane

❀ Step-by-Step Guide

1

Draw a curve in the direction of the arrow.

2

Complete the rear wing of the airplane by drawing trapezoids and triangles.

3

Draw triangle shapes on both sides to create the wings of the airplane.

4

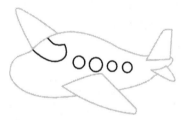

Draw curves and circles inside.

5

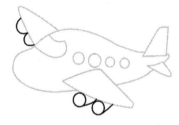

Draw a semicircle on the left. Add a circle and a line to the right.

6

Draw a cute face.

Airplane

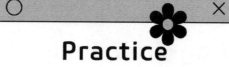

Practice

Draw the entire picture (gray line) following the step-by-step guide

Drawing and Coloring

Aloe Vera

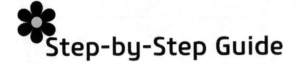

❀ **Step-by-Step Guide**

Normal

1

Draw an incomplete
trapezoid shape with
rounded corners.

2

Draw a rectangular
shape and draw a wavy
line on it.

3

Draw the leaves of
Aloe Vera by drawing
several curves
extending upward.

4

Draw the rest of the
leaves.

5

Create hands by adding
curves to both sides of
the planter.

6

Draw a cute face.

Aloe Vera

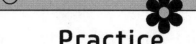

Practice

Draw the entire picture (gray line) following the step-by-step guide

❀ Drawing and Coloring ❀

Cactus

Step-by-Step Guide

 **Normal**

1

Draw a square and draw a long rectangle with rounded corners on top of it.

2

Draw a heart in the center.

3

Connect the elongated half oval on top.

4

Complete the arms by drawing upward curves on both sides of the cactus.

5

Draw cute faces and flowers. Erase the part that overlaps the body.

6

Draw several lines on the body to represent the thorns of the cactus.

Cactus

Practice

Draw the entire picture
(gray line) following
the step-by-step guide

Drawing and Coloring

Castle

Step-by-Step Guide

Normal

1

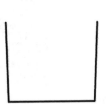

Draw an imperfect square shape.

2

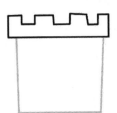

Draw a straight line on top and complete the square zigzag pattern.

3

Draw a heart in the center and a line to represent the door.

4

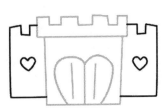

Connect with square zigzag lines on both sides of the castle. Draw a heart in the center.

5

Draw a line upward and complete a small square zigzag pattern.

6

Draw a triangle shape and draw a flag.

Castle

○   ✕

Practice

Draw the entire picture
(gray line) following
the step-by-step guide

Drawing and Coloring

Cloud

Easy

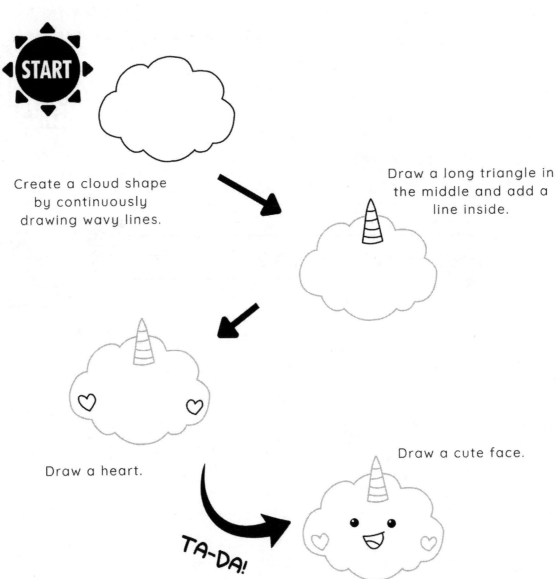

START

Create a cloud shape by continuously drawing wavy lines.

Draw a long triangle in the middle and add a line inside.

Draw a heart.

TA-DA!

Draw a cute face.

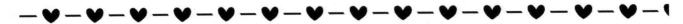

Cloud

Practice

Draw the entire picture (gray line) following the step-by-step guide

Drawing and Coloring

Flower

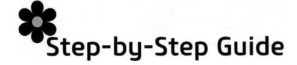

❀ Step-by-Step Guide

Normal

START

Draw an oval.

Draw flower leaves by connecting a semicircle around the oval.

Lower the long curve and draw it in a zigzag shape.

Complete the leaf by drawing curves on both sides and lines inside. And draw a cute face.

TA-DA!

Flower

Practice

Draw the entire picture
(gray line) following
the step-by-step guide

❀ Drawing and Coloring ❀

Mushroom

❀ **Step-by-Step Guide**

Easy

START

Draw a large semicircle with a curled inside and add a curved line inside.

Draw a long oval with a wider bottom.

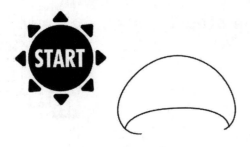

Complete the arms and legs with small half ovals.

TA-DA!

Draw a cute face. Add details by drawing a circle inside.

Mushroom

Practice

Draw the entire picture
(gray line) following
the step-by-step guide

Drawing and Coloring

Rainbow

❀ Step-by-Step Guide

Easy

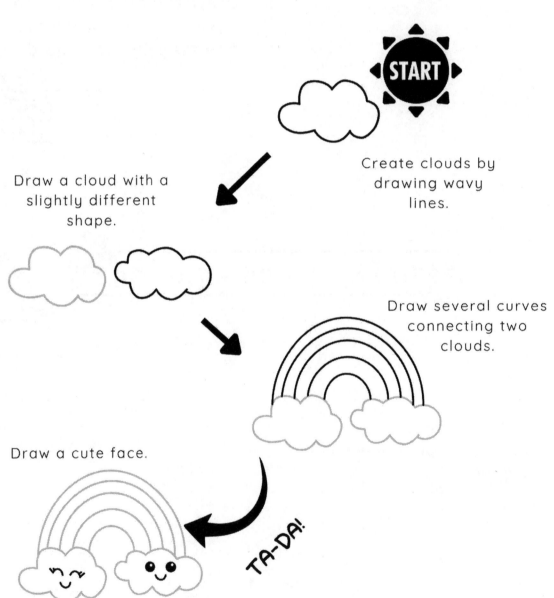

START

Create clouds by drawing wavy lines.

Draw a cloud with a slightly different shape.

Draw several curves connecting two clouds.

Draw a cute face.

TA-DA!

Rainbow

Practice

Draw the entire picture (gray line) following the step-by-step guide

Drawing and Coloring

Rocket

❁ **Step-by-Step Guide**

Normal

Draw the body of a pencil-shaped rocket. Draw a circle inside.

Add the two inner curves. Draw a half rectangle below.

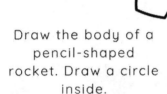

Connect the bent triangles on both sides.

TA-DA!

Draw a cute face. Add zigzag lines to draw the rocket's flame.

Rocket

Practice

Draw the entire picture (gray line) following the step-by-step guide

Drawing and Coloring

Smiling Sun

🌸 **Step-by-Step Guide**

Easy

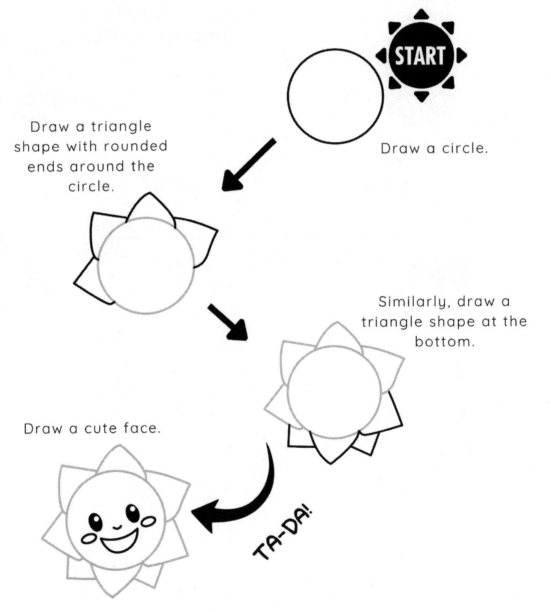

START

Draw a circle.

Draw a triangle shape with rounded ends around the circle.

Similarly, draw a triangle shape at the bottom.

Draw a cute face.

TA-DA!

Smiling sun

Practice

Draw the entire picture (gray line) following the step-by-step guide

Drawing and Coloring

Spaceship

❀ **Step-by-Step Guide**

Normal

①

Draw a semicircle.

②

Draw a curve that wraps around the bottom of the semicircle.

③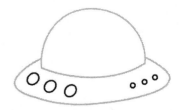

Draw several circles inside.

④

Draw a half-rectangle and a triangle to represent the spaceship's flames.

⑤

Draw a cute face.

⑥

Draw stars around.

Spaceship

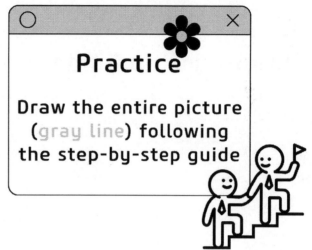

Practice

Draw the entire picture (gray line) following the step-by-step guide

Drawing and Coloring

Snowman

❀ Step-by-Step Guide

Normal

1

Draw a circle.

2

Draw a small circle at the top and erase the overlapping part.

3

Draw a long oval, then add a triangle to it. Finally, draw a circle to finish the hat.

4

Draw a scarf with rounded squares. Add a circle inside the scarf and connect the ends with straight lines.

5

Add lines on both sides to create hands.

6

Draw a cute face.

Snowman

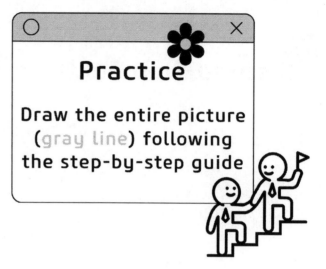

Practice

Draw the entire picture (gray line) following the step-by-step guide

Drawing and Coloring

Avocado

🌸 **Step-by-Step Guide**

Normal

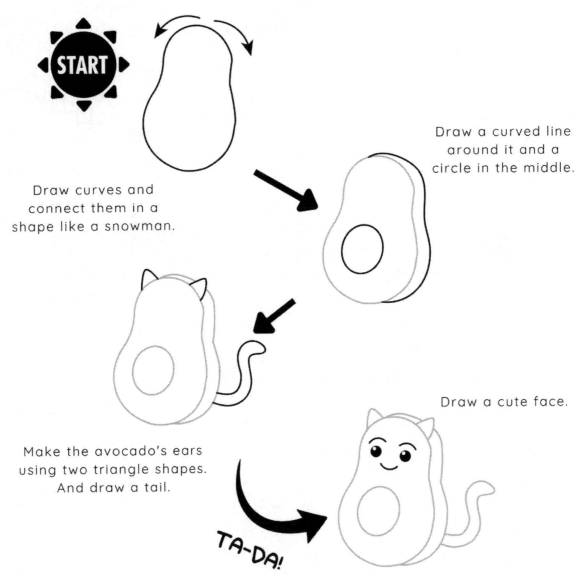

START

Draw curves and connect them in a shape like a snowman.

Draw a curved line around it and a circle in the middle.

Make the avocado's ears using two triangle shapes. And draw a tail.

Draw a cute face.

TA-DA!

Avocado

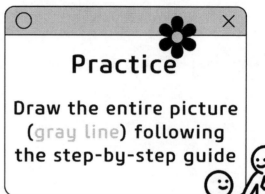

Practice

Draw the entire picture (gray line) following the step-by-step guide

Drawing and Coloring

Banana

🌸 **Step-by-Step Guide**

Easy

START

Draw a curve like a boomerang in the direction of the arrow.

Draw a small oval below. Erase the overlapping parts.

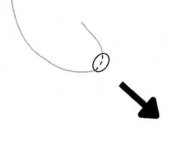

Draw a banana peel in the shape of an '8' in the center. Bend the curve in the middle.

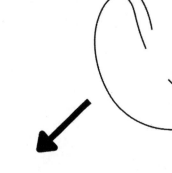

Draw a cute face.

TA-DA!

Banana

Practice

Draw the entire picture (gray line) following the step-by-step guide

Drawing and Coloring

Birthday cake

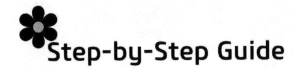

🌸 **Step-by-Step Guide**

Normal

1

Draw an elongated oval.

2

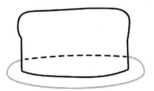

Draw a rectangle with rounded ends. Add some curves while drawing.

3

Draw a cute face. Add a wavy line in the middle.

4

Draw a heart.

5

Draw a square to make the second layer of the cake. Add wavy lines and dots.

6

Draw a candle.

Birthday cake

Practice

Draw the entire picture (gray line) following the step-by-step guide

Drawing and Coloring

Burger

✿ **Step-by-Step Guide**

Normal

1

Draw a wide half oval.

2

Add a wavy line on top of it.

3

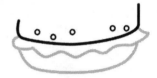

Draw a half square and draw a dot inside.

4

Draw a slightly deeper wavy line on one side (it will be shaped like cheese).

5

Finish the remaining bun of the burger by drawing a half oval.

6

Draw a cute face.

Burger

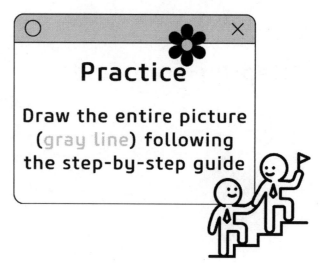

Practice

Draw the entire picture (gray line) following the step-by-step guide

Drawing and Coloring

Carrot

 Step-by-Step Guide

 Easy

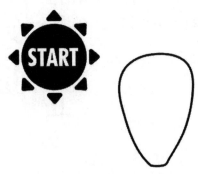

START

Draw an inverted triangle shape with rounded corners and elongated top and bottom.

Draw carrot leaves by making curved lines going up and adding wavy shapes.

Draw a small triangle shape on both sides.

Draw a cute face.

TA-DA!

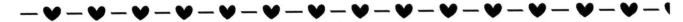

Carrot

Practice

Draw the entire picture (gray line) following the step-by-step guide

Drawing and Coloring

Cherry

 Step-by-Step Guide

Normal

1

Draw a heart shape with blunt ends.

2

Draw an additional heart shape next to it so that it is symmetrical.

3

Add a straight line extending upwards to the top of the heart shape.

4

Draw a leaf shape.

5

Draw a cute face.

6

Add eyebrows to the eyes to make them look prettier.

Cherry

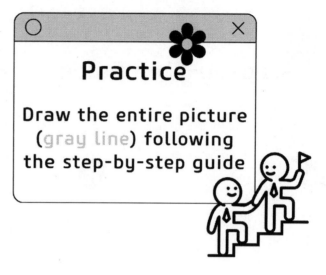

Practice

Draw the entire picture (gray line) following the step-by-step guide

Drawing and Coloring

Chocolate

🌸 **Step-by-Step Guide**

 **Normal**

1

Draw a half rectangle.

2

Connect the oval with zigzag lines to the rectangle.

3

Add an elongated half-rectangle on top.

4

Draw a square shape inside.

5

Create arms by drawing half ovals on both sides.

6

Draw a cute face.

Chocolate

Practice

Draw the entire picture (gray line) following the step-by-step guide

Drawing and Coloring

Cupcake

❀ Step-by-Step Guide

Hard

1

Draw a trapezoid shape and draw a triangular zigzag line on it.

2

Rotate clockwise and draw a wavy line.

3

Add a vertical line inside.

4

Draw a curve in the direction of the arrow and draw a line with a snail shape. Add wavy lines and lines at the bottom.

5

Draw the other side the same way.

6

Draw a cute face.

Cupcake

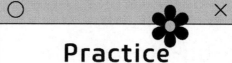

Practice

Draw the entire picture (gray line) following the step-by-step guide

Drawing and Coloring

Dango

 Step-by-Step Guide

 **Easy**

 START

Draw an imperfect square shape and draw an elongated oval underneath.

Draw the same square shape.

Draw the final square shape on top of it and draw a pointed cylinder on top.

Draw a different cute face for each dango.

TA-DA!

Dango

Practice

Draw the entire picture (gray line) following the step-by-step guide

Drawing and Coloring

Donuts

❀ Step-by-Step Guide

Easy

START

Draw a large circle and a small circle in the middle.

Add a semicircle inside the circle and draw a wavy line at the bottom.

Decorate the donuts by drawing stars and lines.

TA-DA!

Draw a cute face.

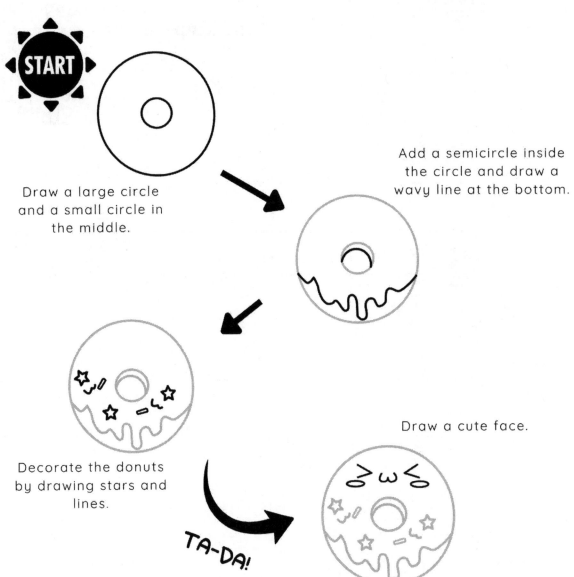

Donuts

Practice

Draw the entire picture (gray line) following the step-by-step guide

Drawing and Coloring

Ice cream

❀ Step-by-Step Guide

Normal

1

Draw an incomplete inverted triangle and draw intersecting lines inside.

2

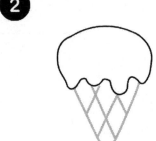

Draw a semicircle and add a wavy line at the bottom.

3

Draw a smaller semicircle with a wavy line, then erase the overlaps.

4

Draw a cherry on top.

5

Draw toppings and a cute face on the inside.

6

Draw a cute face with a tongue out to show a "tasty" expression.

— ♥ — ♥ — ♥ — ♥ — ♥ — ♥ — ♥ — ♥ — ♥ — ♥ — ♥ — ♥ — ♥ —

Ice cream

Practice

Draw the entire picture (gray line) following the step-by-step guide

Drawing and Coloring

Ice cream truck

🌸 Step-by-Step Guide

 **Hard**

1

Draw a rectangular shape and add a little curve to the end.

2

Connect it with a long oval at the bottom.

3

Draw a semicircle and add a circle and trapezoid shape inside.

4

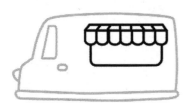

Draw an incomplete rectangle and continuously add wide semicircles on top of it.

5

Draw two circles to make a wheel.

6

Draw the shapes of ice cream and a loudspeaker.

Ice cream truck

Practice

Draw the entire picture (gray line) following the step-by-step guide

Drawing and Coloring

Juice

🌸 **Step-by-Step Guide**

Easy

START

Draw a square shape with some curves.

Draw a cute face, then connect the lines on the sides to shape it into a 3D juice container.

Create a straw by drawing the curve upward and adding lines inside.

Draw an orange by adding circles and dots inside.

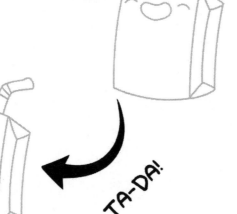

TA-DA!

Juice

Practice

Draw the entire picture (gray line) following the step-by-step guide

Drawing and Coloring

Milk-box

🌼 Step-by-Step Guide

Easy

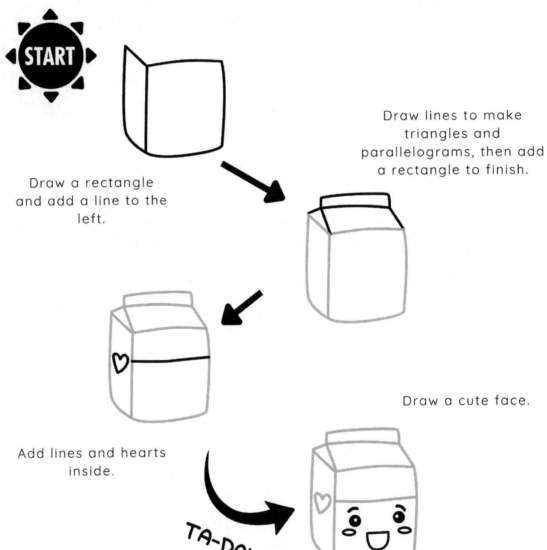

START

Draw a rectangle and add a line to the left.

Draw lines to make triangles and parallelograms, then add a rectangle to finish.

Add lines and hearts inside.

Draw a cute face.

TA-DA!

Milk-box

Practice

Draw the entire picture (gray line) following the step-by-step guide

🌸 Drawing and Coloring 🌸

Peach

Step-by-Step Guide

Easy

START

Draw a wide, slanted heart shape.

Draw a curve following the arrow, then add a long half-oval in the middle.

Draw a cute face.

Draw ovals under the eyes and a curve in the middle of the face.

TA-DA!

Peach

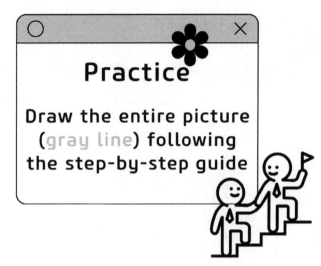

Practice

Draw the entire picture (gray line) following the step-by-step guide

Drawing and Coloring

Pizza

🌸 Step-by-Step Guide

 Normal

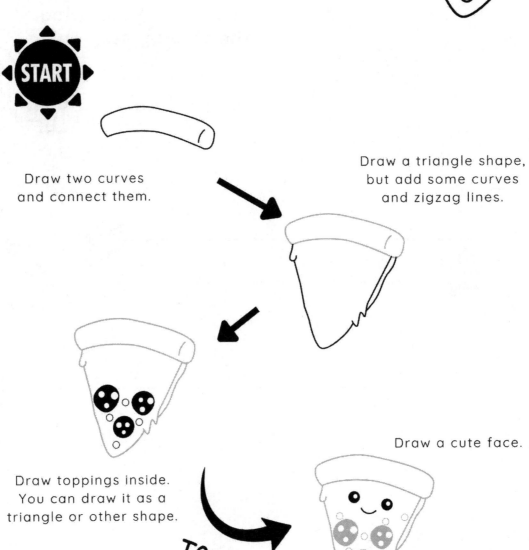

START

Draw two curves and connect them.

Draw a triangle shape, but add some curves and zigzag lines.

Draw toppings inside. You can draw it as a triangle or other shape.

TA-DA!

Draw a cute face.

Pizza

Drawing and Coloring

PopCorn

🌸 Step-by-Step Guide

Normal

START

Draw a square shape and connect a triangular zigzag line on it.

Draw by stacking up wavy lines.

Draw a cute face. Add a heart.

Draw a cloud-shaped wavy line to represent the fallen popcorn.

TA-DA!

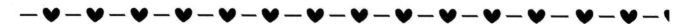

PopCorn

Practice

Draw the entire picture (gray line) following the step-by-step guide

Drawing and Coloring

Strawberry

🌼 **Step-by-Step Guide**

Easy

START

Draw a round, slanted triangle shape.

Draw the bending curve upward.

Draw ovals randomly placed inside.

Draw a cute face.

TA-DA!

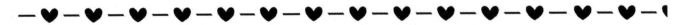

Strawberry

Practice

Draw the entire picture (gray line) following the step-by-step guide

Drawing and Coloring

Watermelon

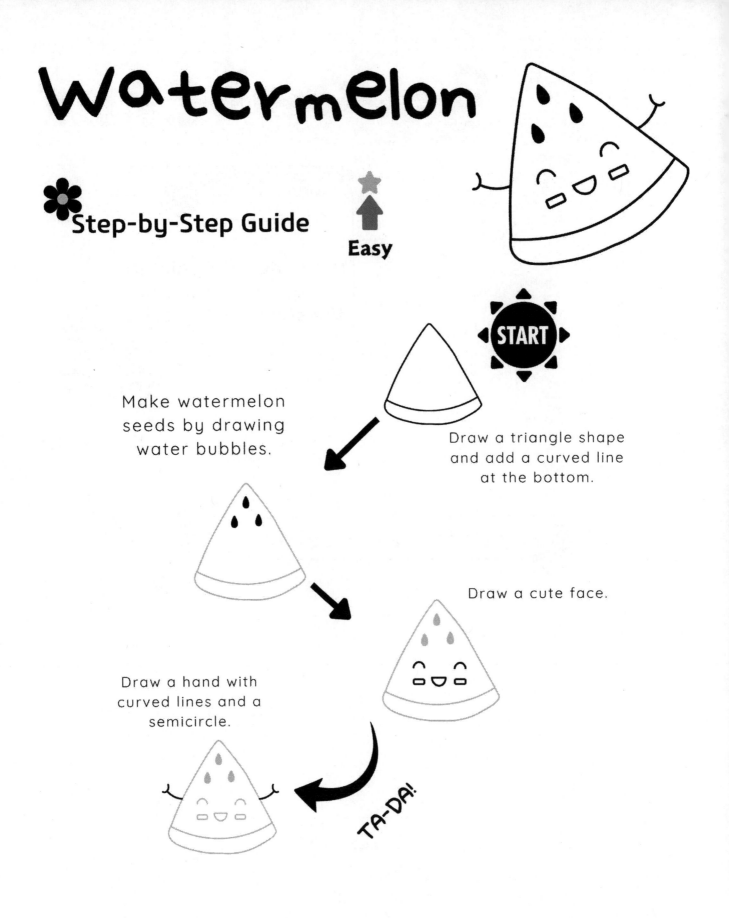

🌸 **Step-by-Step Guide**

Easy

START

Draw a triangle shape and add a curved line at the bottom.

Make watermelon seeds by drawing water bubbles.

Draw a cute face.

Draw a hand with curved lines and a semicircle.

TA-DA!

Watermelon

Practice

Draw the entire picture (gray line) following the step-by-step guide

Drawing and Coloring

Made in the USA
Columbia, SC
12 December 2024